Chapter 2: Understanding the AI Market

Overview of the AI market size and growth

The Artificial Intelligence (AI) market is one of the fastest-growing markets globally, with significant growth expected in the coming years. According to a report by ResearchAndMarkets, the global AI market is estimated to grow from USD 21.5 billion in 2018 to USD 190.6 billion by 2025, at a compound annual growth rate (CAGR) of 36.2% during the forecast period.

Several factors are contributing to the growth of the AI market, including the increasing demand for automation, the availability of vast amounts of data, and the advancements in technology, such as machine learning and deep learning. The increasing adoption of cloud computing and the Internet of Things (IoT) is also driving the growth of the AI market.

In terms of geographic regions, North America is currently the largest market for AI, followed by Europe and Asia Pacific. The growth of the AI market in North America is driven by the presence of a large number of AI companies and the early adoption of AI technology in the region. The Asia Pacific region is expected to grow at the highest CAGR during the forecast period, driven by the increasing demand for AI in the region and the growing investment in AI research and development.

The AI market is highly competitive, with a large number of established companies and startups competing for market share. Some of the key players in the AI market include IBM, Google, Microsoft, Amazon, and Baidu. The increasing competition in the

Chapter 1: Introduction to Making Money Online using AI

Definition of AI

Artificial Intelligence (AI) refers to the simulation of human intelligence in machines that are designed to think and act like humans. It is a branch of computer science that focuses on creating intelligent systems and machines that can perform tasks that normally require human intelligence, such as visual perception, speech recognition, decision-making, and language translation.

AI can be categorized into two main types: narrow or weak AI and general or strong AI. Narrow AI refers to systems that are designed to perform specific tasks, such as image recognition or speech recognition, while general AI refers to systems that have the ability to perform any intellectual task that a human can.

AI systems are built using various technologies such as machine learning, deep learning, natural language processing, and robotics. These technologies allow AI systems to learn from data and improve their performance over time, making them capable of performing tasks that were previously impossible.

AI aims to create systems that can perform tasks that normally require human intelligence and make these systems accessible and useful to people in various industries and applications.

Overview of how AI can be used for making money online

Artificial Intelligence (AI) has the potential to revolutionize the way we make money online. There are various ways in which AI can be leveraged for monetization, ranging from creating AI-powered businesses to using AI in existing online businesses. Here are a few examples of how AI can be used for making money online:

AI-powered businesses: AI can be used to create new businesses that provide AI-based products or services. For example, an AI-powered e-commerce platform that uses machine learning to personalize shopping recommendations for customers or an AI-powered virtual assistant that provides business support services.

AI in e-commerce: AI can be used to optimize and streamline various aspects of e-commerce, such as product recommendations, price optimization, and inventory management. For example, an AI-powered system can analyze customer behavior to recommend products that are more likely to be purchased, or optimize prices based on demand and supply.

AI in digital marketing: AI can be used to improve and automate various aspects of digital marketing, such as target audience identification, ad targeting, and conversion rate optimization. For example, an AI-powered system can analyze customer behavior and demographic data to identify the most effective target audience for a particular product or service.

AI in finance: AI can be used to provide financial services, such as algorithmic trading, portfolio management, and credit scoring. For example, an AI-powered system can analyze financial data to identify investment opportunities and make trades based on real-time market conditions.

AI in content creation: AI can be used to create and distribute content, such as articles, videos, and images, at scale. For example, an AI-powered system can analyze customer behavior to identify the type of content that is most likely to be shared and generate that content automatically.

These are just a few examples of how AI can be used for making money online. The potential for monetization is vast, and as AI technology continues to advance, we can expect to see new and innovative ways of using AI for making money online.

market is expected to drive innovation and growth in the coming years.

In conclusion, the AI market is expected to experience significant growth in the coming years, driven by the increasing demand for automation and the advancements in AI technology. The market offers a wide range of opportunities for companies and entrepreneurs looking to enter the AI space and capitalize on the growth potential of this market.

Types of AI-related businesses and services

There is a wide range of businesses and services related to Artificial Intelligence (AI), which can be broadly categorized into the following categories:

- AI software development: This category includes companies that develop AI software and tools for various applications, such as image recognition, speech recognition, natural language processing, and decision-making. These companies offer AI software and tools to businesses, governments, and individuals looking to integrate AI into their products or services.
- AI-powered products and services: This category includes companies that offer AI-powered products and services, such as AI-powered virtual assistants, chatbots, and customer service bots. These companies use AI technology to provide customers with personalized experiences, automate customer support, and improve customer engagement.
- AI consulting and implementation services: This category includes companies that offer AI consulting and implementation services to businesses looking to integrate AI into their products or services. These companies provide expertise in areas such as AI strategy, AI implementation,

and AI integration, helping businesses to fully realize the potential of AI.

- AI research and development: This category includes companies and institutions that focus on researching and developing AI technology. These companies and institutions conduct research in areas such as machine learning, deep learning, natural language processing, and robotics, and play a key role in advancing the state of AI technology.
- AI data services: This category includes companies that provide data services for AI, such as data collection, data labeling, and data analysis. These companies help businesses to collect and process large amounts of data, which is critical for building and training AI models.

These are the main categories of AI-related businesses and services, and there are many subcategories and niches within each of these categories. The AI market is highly diverse, and there is a wide range of opportunities for businesses and entrepreneurs looking to enter the AI space.

Understanding the target audience for AI-based services

The target audience for Artificial Intelligence (AI)-based services can be broadly categorized into three main segments: businesses, governments, and consumers.

Businesses: Businesses of all sizes, across a wide range of industries, are the primary target audience for AI-based services. AI technology can help businesses automate various processes, improve operational efficiency, enhance customer experiences, and make data-driven decisions. Some of the key industries that are adopting AI technology include finance, healthcare, retail, and manufacturing.

Governments: Governments are also increasingly adopting AI technology to automate various processes, improve public services, and make data-driven decisions. AI technology can be used to improve the efficiency of government agencies, reduce costs, and enhance citizen experiences.

Consumers: Consumers are also a growing target audience for AI-based services, as more and more AI-powered products and services become available. Consumers are using AI technology for personal and professional purposes, such as virtual assistants, chatbots, and customer service bots.

It is important to understand the target audience for AI-based services, as this will help businesses to tailor their offerings to meet the specific needs and preferences of their target customers. By understanding the target audience, businesses can develop AI-based services that are relevant, valuable, and attractive to their target customers, and position themselves for success in the AI market.

Chapter 3: Potential AI-based Business Ideas

AI-powered e-commerce

Artificial Intelligence (AI) is increasingly being used in the e-commerce industry to improve customer experiences and drive sales growth. AI technology can be used in various aspects of e-commerce, including customer engagement, product recommendations, and order fulfillment. Some of the key ways in which AI is being used in e-commerce are as follows:

- Customer engagement: AI-powered chatbots and virtual assistants are being used to provide customers with personalized experiences, automate customer support, and improve customer engagement. AI technology can be used to understand customer preferences and needs, and provide relevant recommendations and support to customers.
- Product recommendations: AI-powered product recommendations are being used to provide customers with personalized product suggestions based on their previous browsing and purchase history. AI algorithms can analyze customer behavior and purchase history to make highly accurate product recommendations, which can help to increase sales and customer loyalty.
- Order fulfillment: AI is also being used to improve order fulfillment processes in e-commerce, by automating various tasks, such as inventory management and delivery optimization. AI technology can be used to optimize inventory levels, predict demand, and optimize delivery routes, which can help to improve efficiency and reduce costs.
- Fraud detection: AI is also being used to improve fraud detection and prevention in e-commerce. AI algorithms can

analyze customer behavior and transactions in real-time to detect patterns and anomalies that may indicate fraud. This can help e-commerce businesses to detect and prevent fraud more effectively, reducing costs and improving customer experiences.

In conclusion, AI is becoming an increasingly important technology in the e-commerce industry, offering a range of benefits to businesses and customers. By using AI technology, e-commerce businesses can improve customer experiences, increase sales, and drive growth, positioning themselves for success in the highly competitive e-commerce market.

AI-powered digital marketing

Artificial Intelligence (AI) is transforming the digital marketing industry, by providing businesses with new and powerful tools to reach and engage with customers. AI technology can be used in various aspects of digital marketing, including customer segmentation, targeting, and advertising. Some of the key ways in which AI is being used in digital marketing are as follows:

- Customer Segmentation: AI-powered customer segmentation is being used to analyze large amounts of customer data, such as browsing and purchase history, to understand customer behavior and preferences. AI algorithms can be used to group customers into meaningful segments, based on common characteristics and behaviors, which can help businesses to target their marketing messages more effectively.
- Targeting: AI is being used to improve the targeting of digital marketing campaigns, by providing businesses with insights into the behavior and preferences of their target customers. AI algorithms can be used to predict customer behavior, such as which customers are most likely to purchase a specific product or service, and target marketing messages to these customers more effectively.

- Advertising: AI is being used to optimize the performance of digital advertising campaigns, by automating various tasks and improving ad targeting. AI algorithms can be used to predict which ads are likely to perform best, and allocate ad spend more effectively, which can help businesses to drive more sales and improve ROI.
- Content creation: AI is being used to automate the creation of digital content, such as product descriptions, blog posts, and social media updates. AI algorithms can be used to generate high-quality digital content quickly and efficiently, which can help businesses to save time and resources, and improve the quality of their digital marketing efforts.

In conclusion, AI is becoming an increasingly important technology in the digital marketing industry, offering a range of benefits to businesses. By using AI technology, businesses can improve their targeting and reach, optimize the performance of their marketing campaigns, and drive growth, positioning themselves for success in the highly competitive digital marketing landscape.

AI-powered customer service and support

Artificial Intelligence (AI) is transforming the customer service and support industry, by providing businesses with new and powerful tools to improve customer experiences. AI technology can be used in various aspects of customer service and support, including customer engagement, support automation, and problem resolution. Some of the key ways in which AI is being used in customer service and support are as follows:

- Customer Engagement: AI-powered chatbots and virtual assistants are being used to provide customers with personalized experiences, automate customer support, and improve customer engagement. AI technology can be used to understand customer preferences and needs, and provide relevant recommendations and support to customers.

- Support Automation: AI is being used to automate various customer support tasks, such as answering frequently asked questions (FAQs), resolving common problems, and processing customer requests. AI algorithms can be used to understand customer requests and provide accurate and relevant responses, improving efficiency and reducing wait times for customers.
- Problem Resolution: AI is being used to improve problem resolution in customer service and support, by automating the process of identifying and resolving customer issues. AI algorithms can be used to analyze customer requests and interactions, and provide relevant solutions and support, improving the speed and quality of problem resolution.
- Analytics and Insights: AI is also being used to provide businesses with insights and analytics into customer behavior and feedback, helping to improve customer experiences and support processes. AI algorithms can be used to analyze customer feedback and interactions, and provide insights into customer preferences, needs, and pain points, which can help businesses to improve their customer service and support strategies.

In conclusion, AI is becoming an increasingly important technology in the customer service and support industry, offering a range of benefits to businesses and customers. By using AI technology, businesses can improve customer experiences, reduce wait times and support costs, and drive growth, positioning themselves for success in the highly competitive customer service and support landscape.

AI-powered virtual assistants

Artificial Intelligence (AI) has revolutionized the virtual assistant industry, by providing businesses and consumers with powerful tools to automate various tasks and improve productivity. AI virtual assistants are being used in a variety of applications, including personal productivity, customer service and support, and home automation. Some of the key ways in which AI is being used in virtual assistants are as follows:

- Personal Productivity: AI virtual assistants are being used to help individuals manage their personal lives and increase productivity. AI algorithms can be used to understand and anticipate an individual's needs, provide recommendations and support, and automate various tasks, such as scheduling appointments, reminders, and email management.
- Customer Service and Support: AI virtual assistants are being used in customer service and support to provide personalized and efficient support to customers. AI algorithms can be used to understand customer requests, provide relevant information and recommendations, and resolve common problems, improving customer experiences and reducing wait times.
- Home Automation: AI virtual assistants are being used in home automation to provide individuals with control over their smart homes, automate various tasks, and improve comfort and convenience. AI algorithms can be used to understand and respond to voice commands, control smart home devices, and provide insights into energy usage and home performance.
- Personalization: AI virtual assistants are also being used to provide personalized experiences, by learning and adapting to individual preferences and behaviors. AI algorithms can be used to analyze and understand an individual's preferences and behavior, and provide relevant recommendations and support, improving the overall experience and satisfaction.

In conclusion, AI virtual assistants are becoming an increasingly important technology, offering a range of benefits to businesses and individuals. By using AI virtual assistants, individuals, and businesses can improve productivity, reduce wait times, and automate various tasks, positioning themselves for success in a rapidly changing technological landscape.

AI-powered financial services

Artificial Intelligence (AI) is transforming the financial services industry, by providing businesses with powerful tools to automate and improve various financial processes, such as risk management, customer service and support, and investment management. Some of the key ways in which AI is being used in financial services are as follows:

- Risk Management: AI is being used in risk management to help financial institutions better understand and manage various financial risks, such as credit risk, market risk, and operational risk. AI algorithms can be used to analyze large amounts of data and provide insights into risk factors, helping financial institutions to make more informed decisions and reduce risk.

- Customer Service and Support: AI is being used in customer service and support to provide personalized and efficient support to financial customers. AI algorithms can be used to understand customer requests, provide relevant information and recommendations, and resolve common problems, improving customer experiences and reducing wait times.

- Investment Management: AI is being used in investment management to help individuals and institutions make more informed investment decisions. AI algorithms can be used to analyze market trends and provide recommendations, helping to improve investment performance and reduce risk.

- Fraud Detection: AI is also being used in financial services to detect and prevent fraud, by analyzing customer transactions and behavior. AI algorithms can be used to identify patterns and anomalies in customer behavior, and alert financial institutions to potential fraud, helping to prevent losses and improve security.

In conclusion, AI is becoming an increasingly important technology in the financial services industry, offering a range of benefits to financial institutions and customers. By using AI technology, financial institutions can improve risk management, customer experiences, and investment performance, positioning themselves for success in a rapidly changing financial landscape.

Chapter 4: Building an AI-based Business

Identifying the problem you want to solve with AI

Identifying the problem you want to solve with AI is the first step in leveraging this powerful technology to improve your business or personal life. Here are some steps you can follow to identify the problem you want to solve with AI:

- Conduct a SWOT analysis: Start by conducting a SWOT (Strengths, Weaknesses, Opportunities, Threats) analysis of your business or personal life. This will help you identify the areas where you can improve and where AI could be leveraged to make a difference.
- Identify pain points: Identify the areas in your business or personal life that cause the most frustration or problems. These pain points could include tasks that are repetitive, time-consuming, or require a lot of manual effort.
- Determine the potential impact of AI: Once you have identified the pain points, determine the potential impact of AI in resolving these issues. How would AI technology change the way you do things and what kind of outcomes could you expect?
- Evaluate the feasibility of AI: Consider the feasibility of using AI to solve the problem at hand. Can AI technology be integrated into your current systems and processes? Are there any limitations or constraints to using AI technology?
- Assess the potential return on investment (ROI): Assess the potential return on investment (ROI) of using AI to solve the problem. How much would you need to invest in AI

technology and what kind of benefits could you expect to see in return?

By following these steps, you will be able to identify the problem you want to solve with AI and determine whether AI is a viable solution. It's important to remember that AI is not a one-size-fits-all solution and that you need to tailor your approach to the specific problem you want to solve.

Conducting market research and identifying your target audience

Conducting market research and identifying your target audience are crucial steps in developing an AI-based business or product. Here are some steps you can follow to conduct market research and identify your target audience:

- Define your target audience: Start by defining your target audience, including their demographic characteristics, preferences, and needs. Consider the age, gender, location, education, income, and other relevant factors that describe your target audience.
- Conduct market research: Conduct market research to gain a deeper understanding of your target audience and their needs. Use online tools, surveys, and focus groups to collect data, and analyze the information you gather to identify trends and patterns.
- Analyze the competition: Analyze the competition in the AI market to see what services and products are already available, and how your product or service will differ from what is already on the market.
- Assess the market size: Assess the market size for your AI product or service, including the potential number of customers, sales volume, and revenue potential.

- Identify customer pain points: Identify the pain points and challenges that your target audience is facing, and determine how your AI product or service can help address these issues.
- Evaluate customer preferences: Evaluate the preferences of your target audience, including the types of products and services they are interested in, the channels they prefer to use to interact with your business, and their preferred payment methods.

By following these steps, you will be able to gain a comprehensive understanding of your target audience and the market you are operating in, allowing you to tailor your AI product or service to the needs and preferences of your target audience. This will help you develop an effective marketing strategy, target the right audience, and increase the chances of success for your AI business or product.

Building an AI-powered solution

Building an AI-powered solution requires a combination of technical expertise and business knowledge. Here are some steps you can follow to build an AI-powered solution:

- Define the problem: Start by defining the problem you want to solve with AI. This will help you determine the scope of the project and set clear goals and objectives.
- Choose the right technology: Choose the right AI technology to solve the problem, including machine learning algorithms, computer vision, natural language processing, and others. Consider the technical requirements, such as data storage and processing power, and make sure the technology you choose is compatible with your existing systems and processes.
- Collect and clean data: Collect and clean data that will be used to train the AI system. This data should be relevant to the problem you are trying to solve, and it should be of high quality to ensure accurate results.
- Train the AI system: Train the AI system using the data you have collected. This process involves inputting the data into

the AI system and allowing it to learn and make predictions based on the data.

- Validate the model: Validate the model by testing it on a separate dataset to ensure it is accurate and reliable. This will help you identify any issues with the model and make any necessary adjustments.
- Deploy the solution: Deploy the solution in your business or personal life. This could involve integrating the AI system into your existing systems and processes, or creating a new platform or application that leverages AI technology.
- Monitor and maintain the solution: Monitor and maintain the solution to ensure it is functioning as expected, and make any necessary updates or modifications to ensure optimal performance.

Building an AI-powered solution requires technical expertise, but it also requires a deep understanding of the problem you are trying to solve and the target audience you are serving. By following these steps, you can build an effective AI-powered solution that meets the needs of your customers and delivers tangible benefits for your business or personal life.

Marketing and promoting your AI-powered solution

Marketing and promoting your AI-powered solution are critical steps to ensuring its success. Here are some steps you can follow to market and promote your AI-powered solution:

- Identify your unique selling proposition (USP): Identify what sets your AI-powered solution apart from your competitors, and use this as the basis for your marketing and promotion strategy.
- Build a website: Build a website that showcases your AI-powered solution and its features, benefits, and pricing. Make

sure the website is easy to navigate, visually appealing, and optimized for search engines.

- Develop a content marketing strategy: Develop a content marketing strategy that showcases your AI-powered solution and its benefits, and targets your target audience. Use blog posts, videos, infographics, and other content formats to educate your audience and build interest in your solution.

- Leverage social media: Leverage social media platforms, such as Facebook, Twitter, and LinkedIn, to promote your AI-powered solution and engage with your target audience.

- Attend trade shows and events: Attend trade shows and events in your industry to showcase your AI-powered solution and connect with potential customers.

- Offer a free trial or demo: Offer a free trial or demo of your AI-powered solution to allow potential customers to test and experience it for themselves.

- Collaborate with influencers: Collaborate with influencers in your industry to promote your AI-powered solution and reach a wider audience.

By following these steps, you can effectively market and promote your AI-powered solution, build a strong brand, and reach your target audience. Remember, marketing and promotion are ongoing processes that require consistent effort and attention, so be prepared to continuously evaluate and adjust your strategy as needed.

Chapter 5: Monetizing your AI-based Business

Understanding the revenue models for AI-based businesses

There are several revenue models that can be used by AI-based businesses. Here are some of the most common:

1. Subscription-based: The business charges customers a recurring fee, such as a monthly or yearly subscription, for access to the AI-powered solution. This is a popular model for SaaS (Software as a Service) businesses, and it provides a predictable and stable stream of revenue.

2. Pay-per-use: The business charges customers based on the number of times they use the AI-powered solution. This model is often used for AI-powered services that are used frequently, such as digital assistants or chatbots.

3. Commission-based: The business earns a commission for facilitating transactions between customers and other businesses. For example, an AI-powered e-commerce platform might earn a commission for each sale made through the platform.

4. Advertising-based: The business earns revenue by displaying advertisements within the AI-powered solution. This model is often used by free or low-cost AI-powered applications, such as mobile games or chatbots.

5. License-based: The business sells licenses to use the AI-powered solution, which can be used by customers for a specified period of time. This model is often used by businesses that sell enterprise-level AI solutions.

6. Data-based: The business earns revenue by selling data generated by the AI-powered solution, such as customer insights or predictive analytics.

The revenue model you choose will depend on several factors, including the nature of your AI-powered solution, the target audience, and the market demand. It's important to consider all of these factors and choose a revenue model that aligns with your business goals and is sustainable over the long term.

Choosing the right revenue model for your business

Choosing the right revenue model for your AI-based business is critical to its success. Here are some factors to consider when choosing the right revenue model:

1. Nature of your AI-powered solution: Consider the nature of your AI-powered solution and how it can be monetized. For example, if your solution is a tool that is used frequently, a pay-per-use model may be appropriate. If your solution is a more complex enterprise-level solution, a license-based model may be more suitable.
2. Target audience: Consider the needs and preferences of your target audience when choosing a revenue model. For example, if your target audience is cost-conscious, a free or low-cost advertising-based model may be attractive. If your target audience values the quality and reliability of your solution, a subscription-based model may be more appropriate.
3. Market demand: Consider the market demand for your AI-powered solution and the competition. For example, if there is a high demand for your solution, a subscription-based model may be more sustainable, while a low-demand market may require a different revenue model, such as a license-based model.
4. Business goals: Consider your business goals and what revenue model will help you achieve them. For example, if your goal is to generate predictable and stable revenue, a subscription-based model may be appropriate, while a pay-

per-use model may be more suitable if your goal is to generate revenue quickly.

5. Scalability: Consider the scalability of the revenue model and whether it can accommodate growth. For example, a commission-based model may be scalable, as it generates revenue based on the number of transactions, while a license-based model may be less scalable, as it generates revenue based on the number of licenses sold.

By considering these factors and carefully evaluating your options, you can choose the right revenue model for your AI-based business and ensure its success over the long term.

Implementing the revenue model

Once you have chosen the right revenue model for your AI-based business, the next step is to implement it effectively. Here are some steps to consider when implementing your revenue model:

1. Plan and design the revenue model: Define the key elements of your revenue model, such as pricing, billing, and payment systems. Consider how you will collect payments from customers and how you will manage customer accounts.

2. Build and integrate the revenue model: Develop the infrastructure and technology needed to support your revenue model. Integrate the revenue model into your AI-powered solution, ensuring that it is easy for customers to use and understand.

3. Test and refine the revenue model: Test your revenue model in a controlled environment and make any necessary modifications. Ensure that the revenue model is working as intended and that it is generating revenue effectively.

4. Communicate the revenue model: Clearly communicate the revenue model to customers and stakeholders, including the benefits and any limitations. Ensure that customers understand how the revenue model works and how they can use it.

5. Monitor and evaluate the revenue model: Continuously monitor and evaluate the performance of the revenue model, making any necessary changes to improve its effectiveness. Consider regular surveys or customer feedback to gain insight into how customers are using the revenue model and what changes they would like to see.

By following these steps and continuously monitoring and refining your revenue model, you can ensure that it is implemented effectively and that it is generating the revenue you need to grow and scale your AI-based business.

Chapter 6: Scaling your AI-based Business

Understanding the challenges of scaling an AI-based business

Scaling an AI-based business can present a number of challenges, including:

- Technical complexity: AI-based solutions are complex and require significant technical expertise to develop and scale. As the business grows, the technology must be able to keep pace, which can be challenging, especially as new and more sophisticated AI technologies emerge.
- Data privacy and security: As AI-based businesses process large amounts of data, ensuring data privacy and security is critical. Businesses must have robust systems in place to protect sensitive data and comply with relevant data privacy regulations.
- Integration with existing systems: AI-based solutions must be able to integrate with existing systems and processes, which can be challenging and time-consuming. Businesses must be able to effectively integrate the AI solution into their existing infrastructure to ensure that it is used to its full potential.
- Skills and talent: Building and scaling an AI-based business requires a high level of technical expertise and skilled personnel. Businesses must be able to attract and retain the right talent to support the development and growth of the business.
- Financial investment: AI-based businesses require significant financial investment, including investment in technology, talent, and infrastructure. Businesses must be able to secure

the necessary funding and manage their finances effectively to ensure long-term success.

- Regulation and ethical considerations: AI-based businesses must comply with relevant regulations and consider ethical considerations related to the use of AI, such as data privacy and algorithmic bias. Businesses must be able to navigate these complexities to ensure that their solutions are used in an ethical and responsible manner.

By understanding these challenges and taking proactive steps to address them, businesses can effectively scale their AI-based solutions and achieve long-term success.

Strategies for scaling your business

Here are some strategies for scaling an AI-based business:

- Invest in technology: Continuously invest in the latest AI technologies and tools to ensure that your solution stays ahead of the competition. This will help you to scale and grow your business effectively.
- Partner with other businesses: Form strategic partnerships with other businesses and organizations that can help you to scale your business. This could include partnering with technology providers, data providers, and service providers.
- Expand your team: As your business grows, you will need to expand your team to support the development and implementation of your solution. Hire skilled and experienced personnel, including data scientists, AI engineers, and business development professionals, to help you scale effectively.
- Focus on customer satisfaction: Ensure that your customers are satisfied with your solution and that they continue to use it over time. This will help you to build a loyal customer base and grow your business over the long term.
- Diversify your revenue streams: Diversify your revenue streams to reduce your dependence on a single source of

revenue. Consider offering a range of AI-based services and solutions to a wider range of customers to maximize your revenue potential.

- Continuously evaluate and refine your solution: Continuously evaluate and refine your AI-based solution to ensure that it meets the changing needs of your customers. Make changes to improve its effectiveness and keep pace with the latest AI technologies and trends.
- Keep an eye on emerging trends: Stay up-to-date with emerging trends and developments in the AI industry to ensure that your solution remains relevant and competitive. Consider attending industry conferences and events, and engage with other businesses and experts in the field.

By following these strategies and continuously refining your solution, you can effectively scale your AI-based business and achieve long-term success.

Examples of successful AI-based businesses and how they scaled

Here are a few examples of successful AI-based businesses and how they scaled:

- Vicarious: Vicarious is an AI company that uses machine learning algorithms to solve complex problems in robotics and computer vision. To scale their business, they formed partnerships with leading technology companies and invested in research and development to continuously improve their AI algorithms. They also hired top AI talent to support the growth of their business.
- Persado: Persado is an AI-powered marketing platform that uses machine learning algorithms to generate more effective marketing messages. To scale their business, they formed partnerships with leading marketing and technology companies and invested in sales and marketing to expand

their customer base. They also hired top AI talent to support the growth of their business.

- Freenome: Freenome is an AI-powered healthcare company that uses machine learning algorithms to detect cancer at an early stage. To scale their business, they formed partnerships with leading healthcare and technology companies and invested in research and development to continuously improve their AI algorithms. They also hired top AI talent to support the growth of their business.
- X.ai: X.ai is an AI-powered virtual assistant that uses natural language processing algorithms to schedule meetings and appointments. To scale their business, they formed partnerships with leading technology and productivity companies and invested in sales and marketing to expand their customer base. They also hired top AI talent to support the growth of their business.

These are just a few examples of successful AI-based businesses and how they scaled. By forming partnerships, investing in research and development, hiring top talent, and continuously refining their solutions, these businesses were able to achieve significant growth and success in the AI industry.

Chapter 7: Legal and Ethical Considerations for AI-based Businesses

Understanding the legal and ethical considerations for AI-based businesses

When starting an AI-based business, it's important to consider the legal and ethical implications of your solution. Some of the key considerations include:

- Data privacy and security: AI-based businesses often rely on large amounts of sensitive customer data, so it's important to ensure that this data is securely stored and protected. Businesses must comply with data privacy regulations such as the General Data Protection Regulation (GDPR) in the EU and the California Consumer Privacy Act (CCPA) in the US.
- Intellectual property rights: AI-based businesses often rely on proprietary algorithms and technology, so it's important to protect these assets through patents, trademarks, and other forms of intellectual property protection.
- Bias and fairness: AI algorithms can sometimes perpetuate existing biases in the data they are trained on, so it's important to monitor for bias and ensure that the solution is fair and equitable for all users.
- Transparency and accountability: AI-based businesses must be transparent about how their algorithms work and how they make decisions. They must also be accountable for any unintended consequences or harm caused by their solutions.
- Ethical considerations: AI-based businesses must consider the ethical implications of their solutions and ensure that they

align with ethical principles such as privacy, security, and fairness.

By considering these legal and ethical considerations, businesses can ensure that their AI solutions are both compliant and responsible and that they have a positive impact on the world. Additionally, businesses should regularly review and update their policies and procedures to ensure that they continue to meet the evolving legal and ethical standards in the AI industry.

Complying with data protection and privacy regulations

Complying with data protection and privacy regulations is an important consideration for AI-based businesses. Here are a few steps businesses can take to comply with these regulations:

- Familiarize yourself with relevant regulations: Businesses must be familiar with the data protection and privacy regulations that apply to their industry and location, such as the General Data Protection Regulation (GDPR) in the EU and the California Consumer Privacy Act (CCPA) in the US.
- Conduct a data protection impact assessment (DPIA): A DPIA is a process used to identify and assess the risks associated with processing personal data. This can help businesses ensure that they are complying with data protection regulations and minimize the risk of data breaches or other security incidents.
- Implement strong data security measures: Businesses must implement strong data security measures, such as encryption and multi-factor authentication, to protect the personal data they process. They must also have a data breach response plan in place to quickly respond to any security incidents that occur.
- Obtain consent from data subjects: Businesses must obtain explicit consent from data subjects before collecting, using,

or processing their personal data. This consent must be informed and freely given, and data subjects must have the right to revoke their consent at any time.

- Regularly review and update policies and procedures: Data protection and privacy regulations are constantly evolving, so businesses must regularly review and update their policies and procedures to ensure that they are compliant and up-to-date.

By following these steps, businesses can ensure that they are complying with data protection and privacy regulations and protecting the personal data of their customers and users. Additionally, businesses must be transparent about their data collection and processing practices and provide clear and easily accessible information to their customers and users about how their data is being used.

Ensuring the responsible use of AI

Ensuring the responsible use of AI is essential for maintaining trust in the technology and avoiding negative consequences. Here are a few steps businesses can take to ensure the responsible use of AI:

- Consider the potential consequences of AI decisions: Businesses must consider the potential consequences of AI decisions, including the impact on individuals, communities, and society as a whole. They must take steps to minimize the risk of harm and ensure that AI systems are used for ethical purposes.
- Ensure that AI systems are transparent and accountable: Businesses must ensure that AI systems are transparent and accountable, and that their decisions can be explained and justified. This helps to build trust in the technology and promotes responsible use.
- Use data from diverse sources: To ensure that AI systems are unbiased and fair, businesses must use data from diverse

sources and take steps to address any existing biases in the data.

- Regularly review and evaluate AI systems: Businesses must regularly review and evaluate AI systems to ensure that they are functioning as intended and are not causing harm. This can involve conducting independent audits, engaging with stakeholders, and seeking feedback from users and customers.

- Foster a culture of responsibility: Businesses must foster a culture of responsibility and encourage employees to consider the ethical implications of AI. This includes providing training and resources to help employees understand the responsible use of AI and promoting a culture of transparency and accountability.

By following these steps, businesses can ensure that they are using AI responsibly and mitigating the risks associated with the technology. Additionally, businesses must be transparent about their use of AI and engage with stakeholders to address any concerns and promote responsible use of the technology.

Chapter 8: Challenges and Opportunities for AI-based Businesses

Understanding the challenges of running an AI-based business

Running an AI-based business comes with its own set of unique challenges, including:

- Data privacy and security: AI-based businesses must ensure the privacy and security of data, as well as comply with data protection regulations.
- Technical expertise: Developing and implementing AI solutions requires a high level of technical expertise and a deep understanding of the technology. This can be challenging for businesses without a strong technical background.
- Scalability: AI-based businesses must be able to scale their solutions quickly and efficiently, which can be challenging as demand for AI solutions continues to grow.
- Integration with existing systems: Integrating AI solutions with existing systems and processes can be challenging, and businesses must take steps to ensure that their solutions are compatible with existing systems and processes.
- Competition: The AI market is highly competitive, and businesses must be able to differentiate themselves from other players in the market to succeed.
- Ethical considerations: Businesses must ensure that their AI solutions are used ethically and responsibly, and that they are transparent and accountable. This requires a deep

understanding of the ethical and legal considerations associated with AI.

- Hiring and retaining talent: Attracting and retaining skilled AI professionals can be challenging, as the demand for AI talent continues to outstrip supply.

By addressing these challenges and taking steps to overcome them, businesses can ensure the success and growth of their AI-based operations. This can involve investing in technical expertise, developing strong partnerships, and building a culture of transparency and accountability. Additionally, businesses must be proactive in addressing ethical considerations and ensuring that their solutions are used responsibly and for the benefit of society as a whole.

Overcoming common challenges

To overcome the challenges of running an AI-based business, businesses can take the following steps:

1. Invest in technical expertise: Businesses must invest in the technical expertise required to develop and implement AI solutions. This can involve hiring skilled AI professionals, partnering with technical experts, and investing in training and development programs.
2. Build partnerships: Building strong partnerships with other businesses, organizations, and experts can help businesses overcome many of the challenges associated with AI. For example, partnerships can help businesses access data, technical expertise, and support to help them scale their solutions quickly and efficiently.
3. Focus on ethics and transparency: Businesses must ensure that their AI solutions are used ethically and transparently. This involves considering the ethical implications of AI and taking steps to ensure that their solutions are used for the benefit of society as a whole.

4. Prioritize data privacy and security: Businesses must prioritize data privacy and security in their AI solutions, and ensure that they comply with all relevant data protection regulations.
5. Foster a culture of innovation: To stay ahead of the competition and overcome the challenges associated with AI, businesses must foster a culture of innovation and experimentation. This involves encouraging and supporting employees to explore new ideas and approaches, and investing in R&D to stay ahead of the curve.
6. Embrace change: Running an AI-based business requires embracing change and being open to new ideas and approaches. Businesses must be prepared to pivot and adapt quickly in response to changing market conditions and technological advances.

By taking these steps and addressing the challenges of running an AI-based business, businesses can ensure their long-term success and growth. Additionally, by prioritizing ethics and transparency, businesses can ensure that their AI solutions are used responsibly and for the benefit of society as a whole.

Taking advantage of the opportunities in the AI market

To take advantage of the opportunities in the AI market, businesses can take the following steps:

- Identify the problem: Identify a problem or need that AI can solve, and conduct market research to understand the potential demand for an AI-based solution.
- Develop a solution: Develop a solution that leverages AI technology to solve the problem, and consider partnering with technical experts and other businesses to help bring the solution to market.

- Target the right audience: Identify your target audience, and understand their needs and preferences to ensure that your AI solution is well-received.
- Build a strong brand: Build a strong brand around your AI solution, and focus on delivering high-quality, user-friendly solutions that are easy to use and accessible.
- Utilize data effectively: Utilize data effectively to drive decision-making, improve the performance of your AI solution, and make it more effective over time.
- Invest in marketing and promotion: Invest in marketing and promotion to help build awareness of your AI solution, and engage with your target audience.
- Focus on scalability: Consider the scalability of your AI solution, and invest in the technical and infrastructure needed to support future growth.
- Keep up with technological advances: Stay up-to-date with technological advances in the AI market, and embrace change by pivoting and adapting to new technologies as they emerge.

By taking these steps and leveraging the opportunities in the AI market, businesses can position themselves for long-term success and growth. Additionally, by developing innovative, effective AI solutions, businesses can play an important role in driving the development and growth of the AI industry.

Chapter 9: The Future of AI-based Businesses

The future growth of the AI market

The AI market is expected to experience significant growth in the coming years. According to market research, the global AI market is expected to grow from $14.7 billion in 2020 to $202.7 billion by 2026, with a compound annual growth rate (CAGR) of 37.6%.

This growth can be attributed to a number of factors, including increasing demand for AI-powered solutions in industries such as healthcare, finance, retail, and technology, as well as the growing availability of data and advancements in AI technology.

In addition, the increasing adoption of cloud computing and the Internet of Things (IoT) is expected to drive the growth of the AI market, as these technologies enable businesses to process and analyze vast amounts of data in real-time.

Furthermore, the increasing focus on sustainability and the need to optimize business processes and reduce waste is also driving the growth of the AI market, as AI solutions are being used to automate and streamline operations and reduce inefficiencies.

Overall, the future growth of the AI market is expected to be driven by the continued development of AI technology, the increasing demand for AI-powered solutions, and the growing availability of data and computing power. As a result, businesses that are able to capitalize on these trends and develop innovative AI solutions are poised for success and growth in the years ahead.

The impact of AI on the global economy

The impact of AI on the global economy is significant and far-reaching. AI has the potential to revolutionize many industries and transform the way we live and work. Some of the ways AI is impacting the global economy include:

Productivity and efficiency: AI is helping businesses automate tasks and streamline operations, leading to increased productivity and efficiency. This can result in lower costs for businesses and higher output for the economy as a whole.

- Job creation: While some jobs may be automated by AI, the development and implementation of AI technologies are also creating new jobs in areas such as software development, data analysis, and machine learning.
- Improved decision-making: AI is being used to analyze vast amounts of data and make more informed decisions. This is leading to better business decisions, improved public policy, and more effective use of resources.
- Economic growth: The growth of the AI industry is driving economic growth and creating new markets. According to market research, the global AI market is expected to grow from $14.7 billion in 2020 to $202.7 billion by 2026.
- Personalization: AI is being used to provide more personalized experiences, leading to increased customer satisfaction and loyalty. This can result in increased sales and economic growth.
- Disruptive innovation: AI is disrupting traditional business models and creating new opportunities for innovation. This is leading to increased competition and the development of new products and services.

Overall, the impact of AI on the global economy is complex and multifaceted. While there are certainly challenges and risks associated with AI, the potential benefits and opportunities for economic growth are significant. As AI technology continues to develop and mature, it is likely to have a profound impact on the global economy in the years ahead.

The future of work in an AI-powered world

The future of work in an AI-powered world is a topic of much debate and speculation. While some experts predict that AI will lead to widespread job displacement, others believe that AI will create new job opportunities and enhance existing ones.

Here are some of the ways AI is likely to impact the future of work:

1. Automation of repetitive tasks: AI is expected to automate many repetitive tasks, freeing up workers to focus on higher-level, more creative work. This will likely lead to increased productivity and efficiency, but could also result in job displacement for some workers.
2. Job creation: As AI technology continues to develop, new job opportunities will be created in areas such as software development, data analysis, and machine learning.
3. Upskilling and reskilling: In order to remain competitive in an AI-powered world, workers will need to continuously upskill and reskill. This will require investment in education and training, but will also result in a more highly skilled and adaptable workforce.
4. Increased demand for human skills: While AI may automate many tasks, there will still be a strong demand for human skills such as empathy, creativity, and problem-solving. These skills will become increasingly valuable in an AI-powered world.
5. Remote work: AI technology will make it easier for workers to perform their tasks from anywhere, leading to increased demand for remote work. This could result in a more flexible and dispersed workforce, but also presents challenges related to collaboration and communication.

Overall, the future of work in an AI-powered world is likely to be characterized by a mix of job displacement and job creation, upskilling and reskilling, and increased demand for human skills. To succeed in this new world of work, individuals and organizations will need to be adaptable, flexible, and proactive in developing their skills and capabilities.

Chapter 10: Conclusion

Recap of the key takeaways from the ebook

In this eBook, we explored the various ways in which AI can be used for making money online, the size and growth of the AI market, and the various types of AI-related businesses and services. We also discussed the importance of understanding your target audience, conducting market research, and building an AI-powered solution that meets their needs.

In terms of marketing and promoting your solution, we discussed the importance of choosing the right revenue model and implementing it effectively. We also explored the challenges of scaling an AI-based business and provided strategies for overcoming these challenges.

Additionally, we discussed the legal and ethical considerations for AI-based businesses, including the need to comply with data protection and privacy regulations and to ensure the responsible use of AI. We also discussed the challenges of running an AI-based business and provided strategies for overcoming these challenges.

Finally, we looked at the future growth of the AI market and its impact on the global economy, as well as the future of work in an AI-powered world.

In summary, the key takeaways from this eBook are:

1. AI has the potential to transform many aspects of the online world, including e-commerce, digital marketing, customer service and support, virtual assistants, and financial services.
2. To succeed in the AI market, it is important to understand your target audience, conduct market research, and build an AI-powered solution that meets their needs.

3. Choosing the right revenue model and implementing it effectively is critical for the success of your AI-based business.
4. Scaling an AI-based business presents challenges, but these can be overcome with the right strategies and approach.
5. Legal and ethical considerations are important in the AI market, including data protection, privacy, and the responsible use of AI.
6. The future of work in an AI-powered world will be characterized by job displacement and job creation, upskilling and reskilling, and increased demand for human skills.

Final thoughts on making money online using AI

In conclusion, the AI market offers numerous opportunities for businesses and entrepreneurs to make money online. With the rapid development and increasing adoption of AI technologies, the potential for growth and success in this field is substantial.

However, it is important to remember that success in the AI market requires a strategic approach, careful planning, and a deep understanding of the target audience and the problem being solved. The ability to build a high-quality AI-powered solution, choose the right revenue model, and overcome the challenges of scaling a business will be key to success.

Moreover, businesses operating in the AI market must be mindful of the legal and ethical considerations, including data protection and privacy regulations and the responsible use of AI. They must also be prepared for the changing landscape of work in an AI-powered world and take advantage of the opportunities it presents.

In short, making money online using AI requires careful planning, a strategic approach, and a willingness to embrace change and adapt to a rapidly evolving market. With the right approach and a commitment to quality, businesses and entrepreneurs can achieve great success in the AI market.

www.ingramcontent.com/pod-product-compliance
Lightning Source LLC
Chambersburg PA
CBHW070318240526
45467CB00046B/1967